The following titles are available at Levels 2, 3 and 4:

Level 2
Baywatch
The Birds
The Canterville Ghost and the Model
  Millionaire
The Cay
Chocky
The Diary
Don't Look Behind You
Don't Look Now
Emily
Flour Babies
The Fox
Free Willy
The Ghost of Genny Castle
Grandad's Eleven
Jumanji
The Lady in the Lake
Little Women
Money to Burn
Persuasion
The Railway Children
The Room in the Tower and Other
  Ghost Stories
The Secret Garden
The Sheep-Pig
Simply Suspense
Slinky Jane
Stealing the Hills
Treasure Island
The Treasure Seekers
Under the Greenwood Tree
The Wave
We Are All Guilty
The Weirdo

Level 3
Black Beauty
The Black Cat and Other Stories
The Book of Heroic Failures
Braveheart
Calling All Monsters
A Catskill Eagle
Channel Runner
Cranford
The Darling Buds of May
Dubliners
Earthdark
Eraser
Forrest Gump
The Fugitive
Get Shorty

Goggle Eyes
Jane Eyre
King Solomon's Mines
Madame Doubtfire
The Man with Two Shadows and Other
  Ghost Stories
More Heroic Failures
Mrs Dalloway
My Fair Lady
Not a Penny More, Not a Penny Less
NYPD Blue: Blue Beginning
The Portrait of a Lady
Rain Man
The Reluctant Queen
Santorini
Sense and Sensibility
Sherlock Holmes and the Mystery of
  Boscombe Pool
St Agnes' Stand
StarGate
Summer of My German Soldier
The Thirty-nine Steps
Thunder Point
Time Bird
The Turn of the Screw
Twice Shy

Level 4
The Boys from Brazil
The Breathing Method
The Burden of Proof
The Client
The Danger
Detective Work
The Doll's House and Other Stories
Dracula
Far from the Madding Crowd
Farewell, My Lovely
Glitz
Gone with the Wind, Part 1
Gone with the Wind, Part 2
The House of Stairs
The Locked Room and Other Horror
  Stories
The Lost World
The Mill on the Floss
The Mosquito Coast
The Picture of Dorian Gray
Seven
Strangers on a Train
White Fang

For a complete list of the titles available in the Penguin Readers series please write to the following address for a catalogue: Penguin ELT Marketing Department, Penguin Books Ltd, 27 Wrights Lane, London W8 5TZ.

My Family and Other Animals

GERALD DURRELL

Level 3

Retold by Joc Potter and Andy Hopkins
Series Editor: Derek Strange

PENGUIN BOOKS

PENGUIN BOOKS

Published by the Penguin Group
Penguin Books Ltd, 27 Wrights Lane, London W8 5TZ, England
Penguin Books USA Inc., 375 Hudson Street, New York, New York 10014, USA
Penguin Books Australia Ltd, Ringwood, Victoria, Australia
Penguin Books Canada Ltd, 10 Alcorn Avenue, Toronto, Ontario, Canada M4V 3B2
Penguin Books (NZ) Ltd, 182–190 Wairau Road, Auckland 10, New Zealand

Penguin Books Ltd, Registered Offices: Harmondsworth, Middlesex, England

First published in 1956
This adaptation published by Penguin Books 1995
5 7 9 10 8 6

Illustrations by Rowan Clifford

Printed in England by Clays Ltd, St Ives plc
Set in 11/13 pt Lasercomp Bembo by
Datix International Limited, Bungay, Suffolk

To the teacher:

In addition to all the language forms of Levels One and Two, which are used again at this level of the series, the main verb forms and tenses used at Level Three are:

- past continuous verbs, present perfect simple verbs, conditional clauses (using the 'first' or 'open future' conditional), question tags and further common phrasal verbs
- modal verbs: *have* (*got*) *to* and *don't have to* (to express obligation), *need to* and *needn't* (to express necessity), *could* and *was able to* (to describe past ability), *could* and *would* (in offers and polite requests for help), and *shall* (for future plans, offers and suggestions).

Also used are:

- relative pronouns: *who*, *that* and *which* (in defining clauses)
- conjunctions: *if* and *since* (for time or reason), *so that* (for purpose or result) and *while*
- indirect speech (questions)
- participle clauses.

Specific attention is paid to vocabulary development in the Vocabulary Work exercises at the end of the book. These exercises are aimed at training students to enlarge their vocabulary systematically through intelligent reading and effective use of a dictionary.

To the student:

Dictionary Words:

- When you read this book, you will find that some words are darker black than the others on the page. Look them up in your dictionary, if you do not already know them, or try to guess the meaning of the words first, without a dictionary.

Before you read:

1 The pictures show two of the Durrell family's homes. Look at the pictures and say what you think.

   a Where is each house?

   b What is near each house?

   c What is the weather like?

   d What can you do in each place? What can't you do?

   e Which house would you prefer to live in?

A   B

2 In the story, Gerald Durrell's family move from House A to House B, on a Greek island. Gerald's father is dead. How do you think the people in the family spend their time in Greece?

   a His middle-aged mother   c His older sister

   b Gerald (about ten years old)   d His older brothers

INTRODUCTION

After July came the cold winds and the grey skies of August. My family had all their usual illnesses. My mother and I had bad colds. My brother Leslie had a problem with his ears. My sister Margo's **spots** were worse than ever. Only my oldest brother, Larry, was healthy, but he found the rest of us very difficult to live with.

'Why do we stay in England in this weather?' he asked Mother. '*They're* ill and *you're* looking older every day.'

'I'm not,' Mother replied. She was reading at the time.

'You *are*,' Larry said. 'We need sunshine . . . a country where we can grow.'

'Yes dear, that's a good idea,' Mother answered, not really listening.

'George says Corfu's wonderful. Why don't we go there?'

'If you like, dear.' It was important to keep Larry happy.

'When?' asked Larry with surprise.

Mother realized her mistake and put down her book. 'Perhaps you can go first and look at the place,' she said cleverly. 'If it's nice, we can all follow.'

Larry looked at her. 'You said that last time. I waited in Spain for two months and you didn't come. No – if we're going to Greece, let's go together.'

'But I've only just bought this house!' Mother answered.

'Sell it again then!'

'That's stupid, dear,' said Mother. 'I can't do that.'

So we sold the house and ran from the English summer.

We travelled by train with our clothes and our most important belongings: Mother's cook books, Leslie's guns, something for Margo's spots, Larry's books, my favourite **insects** and Roger, my dog.

From Italy we caught a boat. We slept when the boat left and then, very early the next morning, we watched for Corfu. The sea turned blue, then purple, and suddenly there was the sleeping island in front of us. We sailed nearer and, above the noise of the ship, we could hear the high, clear sounds of the insects.

PART ONE
THE PINK VILLA

Chapter One

We left the ship and walked towards the town. Larry found two **cabs**, put the bags in one and sat in the second. Then he looked round angrily. 'Well?' he said. 'What are we waiting for?'

'We're waiting for Mother,' Leslie explained. 'Roger's found a streetlamp.'

'Dear God!' said Larry, and then shouted, 'Come *on*, Mother, come on. Can't the dog wait?'

'We waited an hour in Naples for *you*,' said Margo.

'I had a stomach problem,' Larry explained coldly.

'Well, *he's* probably got one too,' Margo replied.

Then Mother arrived and the next problem was getting Roger into the cab. He didn't like the horses, and he didn't want to climb in behind them. In the end we had to lift him up and throw him in while he cried like a baby. The horses were frightened and started moving, and we found ourselves on the floor of the cab with Roger underneath us.

'Really!' said Larry, as we sat up again. 'Everyone's *looking* at us!'

'Stay calm, dear,' said Mother. 'The hotel isn't far.'

Roger put his head over the side of the cab and saw four dirty dogs lying in the sun. The dogs saw him and ran after us. More dogs heard the noise and came to play. When we arrived at the hotel, there were twenty-four animals in the road and Larry was hitting them with his umbrella. He hit Leslie too.

'What are you doing?' Leslie shouted.

'It was an accident,' said Larry. He tried again and knocked Mother's hat to the ground.

We ran into the hotel – the *Pension Suisse* – with Roger in our arms, and shut the door behind us. The dogs continued to make a terrible noise outside. The man behind the hotel desk looked at us. Mother walked towards him, with her hat on the side of her head and carrying my insects. 'Our name's Durrell,' she said calmly. 'I think you have some rooms for us.'

'Yes, Madame,' said the man, watching Roger carefully, 'they're on the first floor.'

3

*'Our name's Durrell,' she said calmly. 'I think you have
some rooms for us.'*

'Then we'll rest before lunch,' she said, and we all went upstairs.

The next morning we started looking for a house with Mr Beeler from the hotel. We drove round the island and looked at **villas** in all sizes and colours. At each one Mother shook her head.

'Madame Durrell,' Mr Beeler said at last. 'What is the problem with all these houses?'

'Didn't you *notice*?' she asked. 'None of them had a bathroom.'

'But Madame,' Mr Beeler replied, 'why do you want a bathroom? Have you not got the sea?'

The next morning we went out without him. Taxi-drivers fought to drive us, and Mother was soon quite frightened by the crowd. We could not understand a word of Greek.

'Can't you *do* something, Larry?' she asked, pushing away the arms of a large driver.

Then we heard a loud voice above the noise. 'Hoy!' shouted the voice. 'Why's don'ts yous have someones who can talks your own language?'

We turned and saw an old American car. Behind the wheel was a short, fat man with a big brown face. He lifted himself out of the car and walked towards us. 'You wants someones who can talks your own language,' he repeated, 'nots these criminals. Just a minutes.'

He shouted loudly in Greek until the other drivers went back to their cars, waving their arms and clearly unhappy. Then he turned to us again. 'Wheres yous wants to gos?' he asked.

'We are looking,' Mother said, 'for a villa with a bathroom.'

The man thought for a minute. 'Bathrooms? You wants a bathrooms? Get into the car.'

The man thought for a minute. 'Bathrooms? You wants a bathrooms? Get into the car.'

We climbed in. While we drove dangerously fast through the narrow streets, our driver talked to us. 'Yous English? English always wants bathrooms . . . I gets a bathrooms in my house . . . Spiro's my name – they alls calls me Spiro Americano because I lives in America . . . eight years in Chicago . . . That's where I learnt my goods English . . . Wents there for good moneys . . . Then after eight years I says: "Spiro," I says, "you haves enough moneys now." Sos I comes backs to Greece . . . brings this car – best ons the island . . .'

We drove along a little white road through the fields and the trees to the top of a hill, and Spiro suddenly stopped the car. 'Theres you ares,' he said, pointing with a fat finger.

Mother opened her eyes for the first time since the beginning of the journey and looked. Spiro was pointing at the side of a hill that came up from the shining blue sea. Half-way up the hill was a small pink villa.

Chapter Two

The villa was small and square in its little garden. The flowers in the garden smelt beautiful and we could hear the sound of insects singing together. As soon as we saw it, we wanted to live there.

Spiro now looked after us. 'Don'ts you worrys yourselfs about anythings, Mrs Durrells,' he said. 'Leaves everythings to me.'

He took us shopping and laughed at the prices until

they came down. He spoke to someone at the bank when our money was late from England. He paid the hotel bill, put our bags in the car and drove us to the house. But Spiro was not just our taxi-driver. He was also our friend. He watched us like a kind uncle, and he loved Mother. 'Be carefuls,' he often said. 'We don'ts wants to worrys your mothers.'

'Why not?' Larry always answered. 'She's never done anything for us . . . why should we think about how *she* feels?'

'Master Larrys, that's not *funny*!'

'He's right, Spiro,' Leslie said seriously. 'She's not a very good mother.'

'Don'ts says that!' Spiro shouted. 'With a mothers likes yours, you musts kisses her feets.'

Now the house was our home, we all started to do the things we were interested in. Margo put on a very small swim-suit and sat in the sun. Larry spent the day in his room, writing; he only came out for meals. Leslie took out his guns and practised shooting at tins in the garden. After one very noisy morning, Larry ran out of his room. 'I can't work like this!' he cried.

'But I've got to practise,' Leslie replied.

'Why don't you take the bullets out of the gun, dear?' Mother asked.

'That's not possible,' Leslie explained, looking at her with surprise. 'I'm trying to hit the tins!'

In the end Leslie moved his tins away from the house.

Mother spent a lot of time in the kitchen with her pots. She talked to herself while she cooked, and the house was always full of beautiful smells. When she was able to leave the kitchen, she worked in the garden.

I also enjoyed the garden, a land of plants and insects. I spent hour after hour on my stomach, watching the secret lives of small animals and learning from them. Roger sat next to me on the grass, clearly bored.

Each day was calm and timeless, and we did not want it to end. But after the night there was a new day, as colourful and unreal as the one before.

Chapter Three

We ate breakfast every morning under the trees. After the coffee, bread and eggs, the family started to talk about their plans for the day. I was not interested in these conversations because I knew what I wanted to do, and I had to finish eating as soon as possible.

'Eat slowly, dear,' Mother said quietly. 'You don't need to hurry.'

Didn't I? Roger and a world of other animals were waiting for me. Together, Roger and I walked and played. He was a perfect friend for an adventure. He watched when I fell and laughed when I stood up again. He sat quietly while I watched a new insect. If I spent too long in one place, he lay down in the shadows and slept.

Roger and I met a lot of people. One of the strangest and most interesting was the Rose-**beetle** Man. I first saw him on a high, empty road, carrying bags of vegetables and boxes of chickens on his back. With one hand he played a pipe and in the other he held pieces of **string**. On the end of each piece of string was a rose-beetle, gold and green in the sun. These beetles flew noisily round his hat, trying to escape from the strings.

When he saw us, the Rose-beetle Man stopped with a jump and lifted his hat. He smiled, touched his pockets and then moved a finger and thumb together. I realized that he wanted money and that he could not speak. So, in the middle of the road, I talked and he used his face and his body to reply. I asked about the beetles. He pointed at the sky and held his arms out. Aeroplane, of course. He pointed at the beetles, then at me to show 'children', and waved the beetles round his head.

The man sat down at the side of the road and opened one of his bags. Inside were six small **tortoises**. My favourite was quite small with bright eyes and a beautiful colour. I asked about the price. The Rose-beetle Man showed me ten fingers, but I knew Greek country ways now and I showed him two. He showed me nine fingers; I showed three. He thought with closed eyes and then showed me six. I offered five. Roger looked bored. The man thought for a minute. Then he gave me the tortoise.

We named the tortoise Achilles. After a few weeks we put him out in the garden, but he always came to us when we called his name. He ate from our hands. Achilles liked people. When we sat or lay down in the garden, he usually fell asleep at our feet. Sometimes he decided to practise climbing on bodies lying in the sun, and then I had to lock him inside.

One day Achilles was not in the garden. We all walked through the trees, calling his name. Finally we found him, dead, at the bottom of a deep hole.

Not long after that I bought a young **pigeon** from the Rose-beetle Man. He was fat and yellow, and Larry gave him the name of Quasimodo. Because he had no

*When he saw us, the Rose-beetle Man stopped with a jump
and lifted his hat.*

parents to teach him, Quasimodo decided that he was not a bird. He walked everywhere, and when we went for walks he ran behind us. He also loved music. If we played songs, he sang; if we played dance music, he danced.

He slept in the sitting-room, and one day we found a white pigeon's egg on the sofa. It was a surprise for us, but it was a surprise to Quasimodo too. He – or she – became wild and difficult and moved into the garden. From time to time we saw her with a good-looking male pigeon.

Chapter Four

Mother decided that I needed a teacher. This was a problem on a Greek island.

'He's all right,' said Leslie. 'He can read, can't he? And I can teach him to shoot.'

'He really must learn to dance,' Margo said.

'Yes, dear,' Mother replied, 'but first he needs French . . . and handwriting – that sort of thing.'

'The child is only interested in one subject,' said Larry. 'Every time I open a **matchbox**, an insect flies out. George could teach him.'

'That's a very good idea,' Mother said happily.

George was a friend of Larry's. He was a very tall, thin man with a deep voice, and he taught me a lot of different subjects. He also showed me how to write down everything I noticed while I was watching animals. I realized that I could learn much more when I wrote things down and studied them.

One afternoon Roger and I went for a long walk in the hills. When we got tired, I lay on the grass and watched the insects. I suddenly noticed small circles in the grass. I touched one, and the circle lifted. It was a door over a hole that went down into the ground. It was beautiful, but what kind of animal made homes like this? I had to know. I called Roger and ran to George's house. When I arrived, there was another man in his sitting-room. I stopped at the door, feeling uncomfortable.

'Good evening,' George said, laughing. 'Do you want more lessons?'

I told George about the little circles in the grass.

'Ah,' George replied. 'Gerry, this is Theodore Stephanides. I think he can help you. Like you, he is a lover of plants and animals. Theodore, this is Gerry Durrell.'

To my surprise, the man stood up, crossed the room and shook hands with me. 'I am very pleased to meet you,' he said. 'Now . . . er . . . there is a kind of spider in Corfu that . . . er . . . builds homes like that . . . Of course, it is possible that I am wrong . . .'

'Perhaps you would like to come and see?' I said hopefully. 'I mean, if it isn't too much trouble.'

'Why not?' Theodore answered. 'I can walk with you now. Thank you, George, for a wonderful tea.' He shook George's hand and put his hat on.

I took Theodore to the place and showed him the little doors.

'Ah ha,' he said, 'yes . . . um . . . yes.' He lifted the door with a small pocket-knife, looked inside and then let the door fall. 'Yes, this is a spider's home, but it's empty. The spider usually hides inside and holds the

He lifted the door with a small pocket-knife, looked inside and then let the door fall.

door with her legs. When an insect walks past, the spider opens the door and catches it.'

We walked silently down the hill, then Theodore shook my hand and said goodbye. He was, to me, a very important person. He knew a lot, and when he spoke to me I did not feel like a child. I liked him for that.

I ran to tell my family about my conversation. I wanted to see Theodore again and to ask him other questions, but I was not hopeful. I was wrong, because two days later Leslie brought a small packet back from town. 'I met your friend,' he said. 'This is for you.'

I looked at the packet in surprise and then I opened it quickly. Inside was a box and a letter.

My dear Gerry Durrell,

*I think this pocket **microscope** will be useful for your studies. It is not a very good microscope, but it will help you with your field work.*

Yours,

Theo. Stephanides

P.S. If you have nothing better to do on Thursday, perhaps you would like to come to tea.

So, for the rest of that summer and the warm, wet winter that followed, Spiro drove me into town every week and I had tea with Theodore.

Chapter Five

As soon as we felt at home, Larry wrote to all his friends.

15

'I've asked a few people to stay for a week or two,' he told Mother one morning. 'We need some intelligent conversation.'

'That's nice, dear,' said Mother, without thinking, 'but I hope they're not *too* intelligent. I can't talk about books and paintings all the time.'

'You don't have to talk about painting,' said Larry. 'But perhaps you can hide some of those terrible detective stories that you read.'

'They're very *good* stories,' said Mother. 'I borrowed them from Theodore. But you must tell the *Pension Suisse* when your friends are coming.'

'Why?' asked Larry with surprise.

'Because they will need rooms, of course,' Mother answered.

'But they're coming here . . .'

'No, Larry, where are they going to *sleep*? There just isn't room here, dear. You must tell your friends not to come.'

'But they're on the way,' Larry said. 'There's an easy answer: let's move to a bigger house.'

'And when they go? What do we do with a larger house?'

'Ask more people,' said Larry, surprised that Mother was so slow.

Mother looked at him. 'Really, Larry,' she said, 'you make me very angry. We are *not* going to move to another house.' She walked out of the room.

PART TWO

THE YELLOW VILLA

Chapter Six

The new villa was very large – a tall, square house with yellow walls, green windows and a red roof. It stood on a hill near the coast. Spiro, of course, found the house and moved everything for us. Larry's friends – writers and painters – came and went.

An old man worked in the gardens and Mother brought his wife into the house to work for us there. Her name was Lugaretzia and she was really only interested in her health. She carefully described every problem that she had. When she arrived, it was her stomach; later, the problem was her feet. She cried when she walked and she cried more loudly when she saw one of us. Larry started eating breakfast in his room after Lugaretzia took off her shoes in the dining-room to show us her toes.

The old wall round part of our garden was a good place for animal-watching. There were day and night workers. The shyest were the most dangerous; when you took away a small piece of the wall, you found a little black **scorpion**.

One day I found a female scorpion with a lot of little babies on her back. I was excited by this new family and

I decided to take them to my bedroom and watch them growing up. I put them carefully into a matchbox and hurried to the villa. Lunch was ready, so I left the matchbox on a table in the sitting-room and went into the dining-room for a meal.

Larry finished eating and went to find his cigarettes. I watched him without thinking while he opened the matchbox. With her babies still on her back, the female scorpion climbed out and walked on to Larry's hand.

Larry felt a movement and looked down. Then he screamed. Lugaretzia dropped a plate and Roger ran out from under the table. Larry shook his hand and the scorpion landed on the table between Margo and Leslie. The babies fell off as she landed, and they went everywhere. The scorpion was now angry and ran towards Leslie. He jumped up, knocked his chair over, and the scorpion ran the other way towards Margo. She screamed. While Mother put on her glasses to see what the problem was, Margo threw a glass of water at the scorpion. The water hit Mother. By this time the scorpion was under Leslie's plate and the babies were running everywhere.

'It's that boy again!' shouted Larry.

'Be careful. They're coming!' screamed Margo.

'We need a book,' cried Leslie. 'Hit them with a book!'

'What's happening?' asked Mother.

'One's coming towards me . . .'

Roger thought that we were in danger. Since Lugaretzia was the only stranger in the room, he bit her on the leg. That did not help much.

When everyone was a little calmer again, all the

Larry felt a movement and looked down. Then he screamed.

babies were hiding under plates, knives and spoons. Since Mother agreed with me that they must not die, the family left the room. I spent half an hour with a spoon, picking them up one by one and carrying them back to the garden wall.

After this, Larry carefully opened all matchboxes with a handkerchief round his hand. Lugaretzia showed us her leg every morning, and Mother decided that I had to start lessons again. George was not on the island at the time and it was not easy to find another teacher, so she asked a Belgian to teach me French. He was a nice man with a small beard and a wonderful moustache. I did not learn any French, but at the end of the morning I was very bored so I enjoyed my afternoons in the country more than before.

Chapter Seven

Spring turned into long, hot summer and the fields turned brown. There was juicy fruit on the trees. The sea was calm and dark and you could see the coast of Albania across the water.

Peter came from Oxford to teach me. He was a tall, good-looking young man with serious ideas about study-ing. This was a problem for me at first but after a few weeks in the sun he became warmer and less serious. He wanted me to write something every day to practise my English. I decided to write a book. Every morning I spent an hour on my story. It was about a journey round the world with my family, and we met every possible kind of animal. One day a big cat jumped

I decided to write a book. Every morning I spent an hour on my story.

down on Mother; the next day Larry fought a dangerous snake. Sometimes it was difficult to save every person in my family at the end of the hour.

While I wrote, Peter and Margo walked in the garden together and looked at the flowers. From time to time Peter felt bad about this and tried to talk to me about numbers, but this did not happen often because Margo got more and more interested in flowers.

As summer continued, we used our little boat to visit a lot of small islands near the coast. But while I fished and studied the sea plants and animals, the family soon got bored. My birthday was near and I decided that *I* wanted a boat. I waited for a good time to speak to Leslie.

'What would you like to give me for my birthday?' I asked.

'I don't know,' he said, happy after a morning of shooting. 'You choose.'

'Well, I really want a boat,' I said.

Leslie immediately realized his mistake. A boat was too big, he said, and too expensive.

'But you asked me! You don't have to buy one; you can make one. Of course, if it's too difficult . . .'

'It's not difficult,' Leslie said quickly, 'but I'll need a lot of time.' He looked at my face. 'Oh, all right.'

For the next two weeks loud noises and screams came from the back of the house.

The day before my birthday, the family drove into town to buy enough food for a party. We decided to ask ten people, but then each of us asked ten. The problem was that these were not the same ten (but we all asked Theodore), so we needed a lot of food and wine. Mother also wanted to take Lugaretzia to the dentist; she was having a lot of problems with her teeth and they all had to come out.

When we returned that evening, the car was full of shopping and Lugaretzia could not stop crying. She could not help with the cooking for the party, but Spiro had the answer.

'Don't yous worrys,' he said. 'Leaves everything to me.'

The next day I opened my presents and then I followed Leslie to the back of the house. There was the most beautiful boat that anyone could want. It was bright green and almost round (because of the size of the wood, Leslie said).

We all carried the boat down the hill to the beach. We had a small bottle of wine. I named the boat *Bootle* and threw the bottle. The bottle landed on the side of the boat and the white wine landed on Larry's head.

Spiro arrived after lunch with a man who, he explained, once worked for the King of Greece. He was there to help with the party.

Visitors began to arrive and the rooms were soon full of people. Spiro's friend carried food and drinks to them. In the kitchen Spiro drank glass after glass of wine while he cooked. Lugaretzia was not much help, but from time to time she stopped to talk to some of the visitors and to show them the inside of her mouth.

More people came and everyone had a good time. Spiro's friend started the dancing and the party continued until morning. It was a wonderful birthday.

Chapter Eight

At the end of the summer I was again without a teacher. Mother was not happy about Margo's feelings for Peter or his interest in Margo. Leslie wanted to shoot Peter; Larry thought about sending the lovers to Athens until they were bored with spending all their time together. Mother did not like either idea and in the end she asked Peter to leave. Margo cried and said that she was ready to die. Spiro's friends watched the coast; Peter must not come back. We all enjoyed ourselves.

Winter came slowly. The shooting season started and Leslie often returned home with bags of dead animals and birds. One day he was telling us about killing one of the birds.

'It was very difficult,' he said at the end.

'Why?' said Larry. 'Shooting is easy.'

'Oh, so you can hit a bird when it's flying, can you?' Leslie asked angrily.

'You just keep your arm still,' said Larry. 'That's all.'

'Right,' said Leslie. 'I want to see *you* shoot something. Tomorrow?'

'Fine.'

The next morning we all went to watch Larry. It was cold and the ground was wet, and Larry said that words were enough; he did not have to *do* anything. We did not listen to him. Larry carried Leslie's gun, and he lifted it and shot at the first bird he saw.

'It's a good idea to put a bullet in the gun,' said Leslie with a smile.

Larry carried Leslie's gun, and he lifted it and shot at the first bird he saw.

'I thought *you* did that,' Larry answered. He put bullets into the gun.

Larry was walking near a shallow pool when another bird flew out. He shot at it and the gun hit his shoulder. He fell back into the pool, and the bird flew away. It took half an hour to pull him out because the **mud** at the bottom of the pool came up to his shoulders.

'Are you all right?' asked Margo.

'I'm fine,' said Larry. 'I'm really enjoying myself. My back hurts, my shoulder hurts, I'm getting a cold, and my shoes are at the bottom of that mud.

When we arrived home, Larry told Lugaretzia to make a big fire in his room and he went to bed with three bottles of wine. After a few hours he was singing happily.

'He's had too much to drink,' said Margo after a visit to his room.

Mother went upstairs. Larry looked at her. 'Who are you?' he asked, and fell asleep.

Early the next morning Margo ran into Mother's room. 'The house is on fire,' she shouted.

Mother jumped out of bed. 'Wake Gerry up!'

Leslie and I ran out of our rooms. 'What's happening?' Leslie asked.

'Fire! Larry's on fire!' Margo shouted in his ear.

Larry was asleep in a room full of smoke. Mother shook him. 'Wake up, Larry! Wake up!'

Larry sat up. 'What's the problem?'

'The room's on fire, dear.'

'Well, put water on it,' Larry said helpfully. 'Margo, you find a large pot . . .'

Larry stayed in bed and gave us orders. When the fire

When the fire was out, the room was full of smoke, burnt
wood, water and empty bottles.

was out, the room was full of smoke, burnt wood, water and empty bottles.

'There you are,' said Larry. 'Easy. Can someone bring me a cup of tea? I've got a bad headache.'

Chapter Nine

Spring came again. The family ate, slept, read and talked. Once a week Spiro brought our post to us and we read our letters to the others.

'Aunt Hermione wants to come here,' Mother said. 'She thinks that the warm weather will be good for her health.'

'No, no!' cried Larry. 'Not Lugaretzia's mouth *and* Aunt Hermione! Tell her that there's no room here.'

'But I told her that we had a big villa, dear,' said Mother.

'We've got to move,' said Larry. 'It's the only answer.'

'Move where?' asked Mother.

'To a smaller villa. Then she can't come.'

'But we can't change villas all the time.'

'It's a good idea,' said Leslie.

'It's very sensible,' Margo agreed.

So we moved house again.

PART THREE
THE WHITE VILLA

Chapter Ten

The new villa was as white as snow. I had new gardens to play in and different animals to make friends with.

One afternoon I climbed a tree and found four soft, fat baby **magpies**. I put the largest and the smallest inside my shirt and climbed carefully down again. When I arrived home, I showed the birds to the family and asked them for names.

'Aren't they *sweet*?' said Margo.

'What do they eat?' asked Mother.

'They're ugly!' said Larry.

'Not *more* animals!' said Leslie. 'What are they?'

'They're baby magpies,' I replied. 'And I want ideas for names, not what you think about them.'

'The things Master Gerrys *finds*!' cried Spiro. 'Whats you calls those birds?'

'Magpies, Spiro,' Mother said slowly and clearly.

'Magenpies,' Spiro repeated.

'Magpies,' Margo told him.

'Thats what I says,' said Spiro, getting angry. 'Magenpies.'

So we called the birds the Magenpies. I built a **cage** for them outside. They were welcome in my bedroom and not in any of the other rooms, but the room that they were really interested in was Larry's. If they came near it, he threw things at them. They decided that he had something to hide.

One day Larry found me in the garden and pulled me upstairs to his bedroom. There were papers all over the floor and holes in many of them. Pens and pencils were everywhere.

'Do something about those birds or I'm going to kill them!' he screamed at me.

I explained that the Magenpies were just interested in things; they didn't know that they were doing anything wrong.

'Lock them in their cage or I'll kill them,' Larry repeated.

The rest of the family heard his shouts and came upstairs.

'Larry, what have you *done*?' Mother asked, looking through his door.

I am not going to answer stupid questions,' said Larry.

'The Magenpies?' asked Leslie.

'Your papers are very untidy. Did they do that?' asked Mother.

Larry looked at her. 'You really are a very intelligent woman,' he said.

Chapter Eleven

Below the villa was a line of fields. I was lying in the fields one day when I noticed a stranger watching me.

'Larry, what have you done?' Mother asked, looking through
his door.

'Where are you from?' the man asked.

'I'm English and my family live in a villa in the hills. Where are you going?' I asked.

'To the sea, to my boat,' he answered. 'And you?'

I wanted to go down to the sea too, so we walked together. 'Where are you from?' I asked as we walked.

'I come from here . . . from the hills,' he said, 'but I am now at Vido.'

This was strange. Vido was a small island near the town of Corfu. Only prisoners lived there, I thought. I told him this.

'That's right,' he said, 'I'm a prisoner. If you're a good prisoner you can build a boat and sail home for the weekend. I must be back there on Monday morning.'

This seemed sensible. I knew that you could not leave an English prison for the weekend, but this was Corfu. I wanted to ask why he was in prison, but I could not think of a polite way to do it. Then we arrived at his boat. There was a very large bird on it. I touched it with my hand.

'Be careful, he bites,' the man said quickly, but the bird did nothing.

'He likes you!' the man said, surprised. 'You can have him if you want. He eats a lot and he bites the other prisoners.'

I did not think about my family. I took the bird.

'I call him Alecko,' the man said. 'Come back here tomorrow and we'll catch some fish for him.'

I said thank you and then I remembered something. I asked about his name and why he was in prison.

'My name's Kosti,' he said, 'Kosti Panopoulos. I killed my wife.' He pushed his boat into the water and climbed in. 'Until tomorrow!' he called.

'My name's Kosti,' he said, 'Kosti Panopoulos. I killed
my wife.'

It was a long walk home because Alecko was very heavy. Mother and Margo met me at the door. 'What's *that*?' asked Mother.

'It's very big,' said Margo.

The others came to see the new bird. Alecko looked at them and started moving his mouth.

'It's dangerous,' said Larry.

'Where are you going to keep him?' Mother asked.

I decided to make the Magenpies' cage into two. Mother thought that this was a good idea.

'Where did you get it?' Leslie asked.

I explained about my meeting with Kosti and, without thinking, about the prison on Vido. I told them about Kosti's weekend visits and our plan to go fishing.

'I don't like the idea, dear,' Mother said. 'You don't know what he did.'

'Yes I do!' I said. 'He killed his wife.'

'A *murderer*!' Mother cried. 'And he walks round in the fields. Gerry, you mustn't go fishing with him.'

In the end she agreed that I could go if Leslie came and looked at the man first. So after the next day's fishing I had plenty of food for Alecko.

Chapter Twelve

The house was busy. Farmers arrived with bags of fruit, vegetables and chickens. Margo lay on the dining-room floor and made large pictures on brown paper. Leslie stood in the middle of pieces of furniture, trying to decide where to put them. Mother cooked in the kitchen with the help of two local girls. I went from room to room and helped if I could. Upstairs in his bedroom Larry was asleep. The family was getting ready for a party.

When the day arrived, I found that some of my snakes in the pool outside were killing the fish. I moved the snakes to a large tin. A little later I noticed that the tin was in the sun and the snakes were lying on the top of the water without moving. They looked dead. I ran into the house with them. The only way to save them, I explained to Mother, was to put them in a cold bath. Mother agreed and the snakes soon looked better.

I left them there and went outside again to look at the tables. In the middle of a beautiful dish of food sat the Magenpies. There were knives and forks everywhere, and bottles of beer lay in pieces on the ground. One of the birds walked slowly towards me with a flower in his mouth and fell off the table. They were both full of beer.

Mother came out. After a few angry words she was calmer. 'You must close their cage, dear. Well, I can't really be angry with them if they've drunk too much. They don't know what they're doing.'

I took the Magenpies back to their cage and of course Alecko was not there either. I hoped that he was on the beach and that he planned to stay there.

The first visitors arrived. Leslie came out of the trees after a few hours of shooting and went into the house. Suddenly there was a shout.

'What's the matter with Leslie?' asked Mother.

He arrived in the garden wearing only a small towel. The visitors all looked at him.

'What's the matter, dear?' Mother asked.

35

'Snakes!' shouted Leslie. 'The *bath* is full of *snakes*.'

'Why don't you put some clothes on, dear . . .'

'Great big snakes . . .'

'I agreed that Gerry could put them there, dear. I'm sorry. They were very sick.' Mother turned to the visitors to explain.

'Really, Mother!' said Larry.

'Don't *you* start,' said Mother. 'Leslie was the one in the bath with the snakes, not you.'

'Am I going to have a bath or not?' Leslie asked.

'All right,' said Mother. 'Gerry, take the snakes out of the bath and put them in a pot or something.'

'Outside!' Leslie shouted.

'Don't shout, dear, don't shout!'

When I returned to the garden, Larry was explaining everything to the visitors. 'There are animals in every corner of the house,' he was saying. 'There are dangerous scorpions and wild magpies. There's danger at any time of the day or night . . .'

'Well,' said Mother quickly, 'lunch is ready.'

Everyone sat down happily. Then two of the visitors screamed and jumped out of their chairs.

'Oh dear, now what's happened?' Mother asked.

'It's probably scorpions again,' Larry said.

The only person who was brave enough to look under the table was Theodore. 'Ah!' he said. 'It seems to be a large black and white bird.'

'Gerry, catch that bird!' Larry ordered. 'The soup's getting cold.'

Alecko was not happy. I fought with him under the table, and when he was back in his cage I was hot and tired.

'*Snakes!*' *shouted Leslie. '*The* bath *is full of* snakes.'

We ate and we drank. After that the visitors were too full to do anything but lie and rest in the garden. Tea was another wonderful meal, and then we all lay on the grass again and night fell. The sky was soft and black. The smell of the flowers was beautiful.

THE RETURN

In the end Mother realized that I needed some real lessons. She decided to take us back to England. The family was not happy, but one day we said goodbye to our friends and left the villa.

When we arrived at the ship, Spiro shook our hands without speaking. Then he stood and looked at us. 'Wells, goodbyes,' he said, and he started to cry. 'I didn't wants to cry,' he said, 'but you're likes my familys.'

We climbed on to the ship and started across the sea. Corfu slowly disappeared and we were all very sad. We sat silently in the train while it crossed Italy and Switzerland. Above our heads the Magenpies talked and Alecko screamed. Roger lay at our feet.

When we left Switzerland, a man came to look at our passports. He gave them back to Mother with a piece of paper. Mother read it. 'Look at this!' she said angrily.

Larry looked at the paper and laughed. On the paper, under *Description of Passengers*, were the words: *One travelling **zoo***.

The train continued towards England.

EXERCISES

Vocabulary Work

Have you understood these words from the story?

spots	*insects*	*villas*	*cabs*	*beetle*
tortoises	*pigeon*	*matchbox*	*microscope*	*scorpion*
mud	*magpies*	*cage*	*zoo*	*string*

1 Write some of the words in the right places

   a BUILDINGS: farm, . . .

   b BIRDS: . . ., . . .

   c . . . : spider, . . .

   d ANIMALS: . . ., . . .

2 Which word means something that:

   a you can travel in?   f makes you dirty?

   b you buy matches in?   g grows on your skin?

   c you look through?   h you can keep birds in?

   d you can tie things together with?

   e people visit to see wild animals?

Comprehension

Part One

1 Which of these are people? Which are animals? Explain who or what each one is.

   a Roger   d Spiro   g Larry

   b George   e Achilles   h Leslie

   c Margo   f Theodore   i Quasimodo

Part Two

2 Explain why:

    a Larry started eating his breakfast in his bedroom.

    b Roger bit Lugaretzia.

    c Leslie built a boat.

    d Mother asked Peter to leave Corfu.

    e Larry fell into a pool.

    f the family moved house again.

Part Three

3 Answer the questions about this sentence from the story: 'The *bath* is full of *snakes*.'

    a Who is speaking?

    b How does he feel?

    c What is he wearing?

    d Who is listening to him?

    e Why are there snakes in the bath?

    f How does the problem end?

    g What happens next?

Discussion

1 Why do you think Gerald Durrell called his book *My Family and Other Animals*? Would you like to be part of a family like his? Why (not)?

2 When Mother decided that Gerald needed lessons, everyone in the family had a different idea. Read their ideas again (see page 12). Do you agree with any of them? What kind of lessons do you think he really needed?

Writing

1 Explain in about 150 words why the Durrells moved house so many times.

2 Write a letter from one person in the family to a friend in England. In about 200 words, describe the good things about life in Corfu.

3 Which part of the story did you think was the funniest? Write what happened in about 150 words.